F-4
Phantom II

F-4
Phantom II
Tony Holmes

OSPREY
AEROSPACE

Published in 1990 by Osprey Publishing
Limited
59 Grosvenor Street, London W I X 9DA

© Osprey Publishing Limited 1991

British Library Cataloguing in Publication
Data

Holmes, Tony
    F-4 Phantom II
    1. United States, Military, Fighter
aeroplanes, history
    I. Title II, Series
    623.746409

ISBN 1855 32 1254

Designed by Paul Kime
Printed in Hong Kong

Front cover Not exactly flying a tactical
formation over the snow-capped Sierra
Nevada Mountains, this pair of RF-4s
nevertheless still 'look the business' in this
March 1983 shot. An extremely rare
version of the Phantom II, only 46 RF-4Bs
were built at St Louis in two separate
batches, the first between May 1965 and
December 1966, and the second from
January to December 1971. Differing only in
the wings used (the later batch had the
slightly bulged F-4J style wing), all 46 RF-4s
were fitted out with essentially the same
camera equipment as that installed in the
more common US Air Force RF-4C. Flown
in Vietnam by VMCJ-1, two other Marine
Composite squadrons (VMCJ-2 and -3) also
flew the RF-4B before they were all
amalgamated into VMFP-3 at El Toro in July
1975. Steadily upgraded over the years, the
surviving RF-4s were heavily overhauled at
the Naval Air Rework Facility (NARF) at
North Island in 1978 during a programme
entitled the Sensor Update and
Refurbishment Effort (SURE). New systems
installed in the RF-4 included the
AN/ASN-92(V) Intertial Navigation Set,
AN/ASW-25B Datalink, AN/AAD-5
Infrared Reconnaissance Set, AN/APD-10
Sideways-Looking Airborne Radar (SLAR)
and the AN/AP-202 Radar Beacon
(*Frank B Mormillo*)

Backcover Slats and flaps lowered and
tailhook firmly locked down an F-4J from
VF-74 prepares to embrace the deck of USS
Forrestal (CV-59) once more. Cruising in the
calmer waters of the Med when this photo
was taken in October 1977, the *Forrestal*
had just welcomed VF-74 back aboard after
an absence of two years while the squadron
was detached to CVW-8 aboard the USS
Nimitz (CVN-68) (*Angelo Romano*)

Title page Wearing distinctive Maltese
crosses on its wingtips and fuselage, this
RF-4E can belong to only one air force, the
German Luftwaffe. The largest operator of
export recce-Phantom IIs, the Germans
purchased a total of 88 RF-4Es under the
Peace Rhine programme which
started in January 1971. Belonging to
Aufklarungsgeschwader 52 (AKG 52), this
particular RF-4 (35+77) is closing on a
KC-135 over Germany in November 1982.
The 77th RF-4E delivered, this Phantom II
still wears its original grey/green splinter
camouflage scheme (*Peter R Foster*)

Half title page Painted up in traditional
Commander Air Group (CAG) colours, an
early production F-4J of VF-151 'Fighting
Vigilantes' cruises in towards Naval Air
Facility (NAF) Atsugi, Japan, in June 1978.
The rainbow colours associated with the
'bosse's' aircraft have been a part of US
naval aviation since the early 1950s, these
special schemes only disappearing with the
advent of low-viz greys in the early 1980s.
Along with the rest of VF-151's F-4Js, this
aircraft returned to NAS North Island,
California, for upgrading to F-4S specs soon
after this photo was taken
(*Masumi Wada via Angelo Romano*)

Contents

Right Having the double distinction of being the only fast jet on base that is not painted in low-viz colours, and being the only VMFA-212 'Lancers' F-4S in the Hawaiian Islands, this preserved Phantom II guards the flight line at Marine Corps Air Station (MCAS) Kaneohe Bay. Equipped with the F-4 for over 20 years, the 'Lancers' finally traded in their venerable Phantom IIs for brand new F/A-18C Hornets in mid-1989. This aircraft, an early F-4S, has been sprayed up as the bosse's Phantom II, Colonel Gary 'Filthy' Elsten's name taking pride of place on the canopy rail (*Steve Mansfield*)

The 'Anchored' Ghosts

Of all the military hardware in operation today arguably the most impressive is the behemoth US Navy aircraft carrier. Capable of launching a large 'Alpha Strike' in any weather, anywhere, the carrier air wing is a military asset that has been nurtured and developed over the decades to its present level of slick sophistication. Although operating the best aircraft money can buy in the 1990s, 30 years ago the carrier air wing was most definitely the 'poor relation' to land-based air forces. Flying underpowered aircraft with a limited range, the average Navy pilot often cast a sideways glance at his Mach 2 compatriot in the USAF. Distinguished by their unsavoury deck manners, types like the Fury, Skyray, Cutlass and the deadly Demon were generally overweight, unruly beasts, who usually proved more lethal to their pilots than to any potential enemy.

However, toiling away in the McDonnell design department in St Louis, Missouri, were a team of highly gifted individuals whose collective efforts would enable US naval aviators to take on the best of the best and win by the mid 1960s. Led by Herman D Barkey, the McDonnell team designed the F4H-1, or Phantom II as it is better known, specifically to a US Navy requirement for a 'do-it-all', in any weather, fighter. A classic almost from the time of its first flight in May 1958, over 5200 Phantom IIs were to take to the skies over the next 23 years. Flown by over 20 US Navy fighter squadrons during its quarter-century of service to the fleet, the Phantom II proved to be the backbone of many air wings in Vietnam, plus the workhorse during more peaceful cruises with the Third, Sixth and Seventh Fleets after 1973. Finally phased out of frontline Navy service in 1986, the 'anchored' Phantom II is now but a memory for aviation enthusiasts the world over. However, the following chapter will hopefully serve as a brief tribute to both the Phantom II and the naval aviators who flew the 'beautiful' bent-winged beast from carrier decks in the 1960s, 70s and 80s.

Well in the groove for a 'three-wire', the pilot gently drifts across the ramp of the carrier towards the looming grey mass of the flightdeck. A classic shot taken in late 1961, this F-4B Phantom II, letting it 'all hang out', belonged to VF-101 'Grim Reapers', the very first squadron to receive the new McDonnell fighter on the east coast. Charged with the responsibility of training a new breed of pilot and radar intercept officer (RIO), VF-101's task was a daunting one. Led by Lieutenant Commander Gerald G O'Rourke, VF-101 set up shop at Naval Air Station Key West, Florida, in late 1959, although its first F4H-1s (or F-4As and Bs as they were designated in September 1962) did not arrive until early 1961. Only the third F-4B ever built, this Phantom II (BuNo 148366) has a cream-coloured radome (seen on early production Bravo-model aircraft) which houses the 32-inch radar dish antennae for the Westinghouse APQ-72 system, the brain of the early model F-4 (*Photo US Navy via David F Brown*)

Right Could this F-4J be the personal mount of the highest ranking Soviet RIO in the US Navy, one wonders? Looking down from *Forrestal*'s island, the 'rear office' of this VF-74 jet is clearly visible. The scope for the APQ-59 radar and AWF-10 pulse-doppler fire control system can be seen at the base of the instrument panel, as can the pull rings for the Martin-Baker Mk H7 ejector seat. The port bleed air louvre assembly and intake ramp can also be picked out adjacent to the rear cockpit (*Angelo Romano*)

Above The first of over 20 frontline squadrons to receive the F-4 was VF-74 'Be-devilers' who, under the leadership of Commander Julian S Lake, received their first Phantom IIs in July 1961. Working closely with VF-101, the squadron virtually wrote the operational manual for the F-4B over the next 12 months, first taking the aircraft to sea on board the USS *Saratoga* (CV–60) in October 1961 for sea qualifications, and then departing on a Mediterranean cruise on board USS *Forrestal* (CV–59) in August 1962. This photo however, shows the squadron equipped with the more potent F-4J exactly ten years later as they, and the rest of CVW-8 on board the USS *America* (CV-66), cruise in the Tonkin Gulf off the North Vietnamese coast. Rushed away from a routine visit to the Med, the *America* was hurriedly despatched to WestPac soon after the North Vietnamese escalated hostilities. Unusually, VF-74 were the only Navy fighter squadron on the *America*, MiG CAP duties being shared with VMFA-333 'Shamrocks', a US Marine Corps F-4J unit from MCAS Beaufort, South Carolina. Carrying a centreline McDonnell 600 US gallon tank and only a single AIM-9G Sidewinder, this aircraft, in the process of being firmly secured to the catapult, is soon to depart on a training sortie. The yellow-vested flight director in the foreground instructs the crew on the progress of the catapult attachment through hand signals (*US Navy via David F Brown*)

Above Fully armed, the CAG's F-4J is slowly towed back to 'fighter country' on board the brand new USS *Nimitz* (CVN-68). Temporarily part of CVW-8 again for *Nimitz*'s maiden voyage with the Sixth Fleet, VF-74, and sometimes sister-squadron VMFA-333, cruised the Med during the Bicentennial year of 1976. Since the squadron's last cruise as part of CVW-8, the 'Be-devilers' had drastically altered their tail markings, a highly stylized demon's head now taking pride of place on the fins of VF-74 F-4Js. BuNo 153784 also wore patriotic colours on its rudder, although the more common rainbow shades associated with CAG aircraft of the 1970s were a surprise omission from the fin of this F-4 (*Angela Romano*)

Left Time to strap on an F-4J! Sitting pretty in the front office of a veteran VF-31 'Tomcatters' Phantom II is an equally seasoned naval aviator, the CAG of CVW-3. Having stuffed his sheath of flight notes and maps down the side of the instrument panel coaming, CAG reaches back for his shoulder harness straps. Meanwhile, his RIO briefly surveys the situation before easing himself into the jet (*Angelo Romano*)

Above left Tramping down the deck of USS
Saratoga (CV-60), TOMCATTER 103 nears
terminal velocity of 150 knots as it shoots
off waist cat one. An F-4J operator for 12
years, VF-31 spent much of that time aboard
the '*Super Sara*', embarking on no less than
11 cruises with CVW-3 until the squadron
transitioned from the Phantom II to the
Tomcat in 1980. This particular aircraft
(BuNo 155841) was part of the largest
production batch of F-4Js in a mid series
group built in 1968–69. A total of 522 J-
models were delivered to the US Navy and
Marine Corps between 1966 and January
1972 (*Angela Romano*)

Below left High above the Med in October
1977, a VF-31 F-4J maintains a fluid deuce
formation with the photo-ship, another
'Tomcatters' Phantom II. A unit with a long
and proud history, VF-31 is actually the
second-oldest US Navy fighter squadron in
existence. For many years designated
VF-3A, the unit was renumbered VF-31 in
August 1948 and equipped with the
pugnacious F8F Bearcat. During the 1950s
VF-31 flew Panthers, Banshees and Demons
before commencing operations with the
F-4B in early 1964, the venerable Phantom II
staying on the squadron books for the next
17 years (*Angelo Romano*)

Above Coming in close for a good look at
the photographer, the pilot eases his rather
blotchy F-4J towards the camera. As stated
on the spine of the aircraft, this Phantom II
belongs to VF-33 'Tarsiers', the very first
unit to receive the J-model F-4. However,
that event took place ten years before this
photo was taken over the Med in October
1977. Part of CVW-7 assigned to USS
Independence (CV-62), this particular VF-33
F-4J totes a pair of triple ejector racks
(TERs), complete with blue 25 lb practice
bombs, under each wing. Unusually, this
'Tarsiers' aircraft has no triple digit modex
on the nose. This particular Med cruise was
the last of six straight deployments the
squadron had made since 1970 with CVW-7
on board the *Independence*. The 'Tarsiers',
or 'Starfighters' as they are now known,
eventually traded in the F-4Js for F-14s in
late 1981 (*Angelo Romano*)

Left Milli-seconds away from slamming back aboard the steel deck of USS *America* (CV-66), a rather smart looking VF-142 'Ghostriders' F-4J glides over the stern of the supercarrier. Eight months before this shot was taken in March 1974 the squadron had just completed its seventh, and last, war cruise over Vietnam with CVW-14. Weary combat veterans with five MiG kills to their credit, VF-142 were transferred to more peaceful waters, and CVW-8, for a single Med cruise on board the *America*. Along with a change in coasts came a change in colours, this flashy scheme only lasting a single cruise. Back at NAS Miramar by August, the squadron soon started the transition onto the mighty Tomcat (*Angelo Romano*)

Above Wearing perhaps the snappiest scheme ever to adorn a Phantom II radome, a gleaming F-4S from VF-21 'Freelancers' heads up a mixed line of Navy fighters at the 1980 NAS Miramar open house. A rather unique Phantom II operator, VF-21 flew no less than four different versions of the F-4 between 1963 and 1983. The S-model was only briefly associated with the squadron, however, as this variant was deemed unsuitable for operations from the small USS *Coral Sea* (CV-43), VF-21's home at the time. Rather surprisingly, VF-151 and -161 re-equipped with the F-4S soon after the 'Freelancers' reformed on the less sophisticated N-model, and took the aircraft to sea aboard USS *Midway* (CV-41), *Coral Sea*'s sister ship! In earlier times, VF-21 had won its battle spurs flying F-4Bs and Js during seven combat cruises off the coast of Vietnam aboard several carriers (*Frank B Mormillo*)

For as long as aircraft have operated from carrier decks VF-111 'Sundowners' have adorned them with shark mouths! Sporting a tasty pair of gnashers, this particular F-4N was the personal mount of the then head-'Sundowner', Commander John Brickner. Having just returned from its 1974/75 WestPac cruise on board the *Coral Sea*, the squadron had been involved in covering the final evacuation of South Vietnam and Cambodia. The ram air intake for the cockpit air conditioning system has also been 'attacked' by the squadron paint shop, although the relevance of the four back rectangles is a mystery. Perhaps it denotes the 'four' war cruises undertaken by VF-111 with the F-4B. Having already completed seven WestPacs with various versions of the beautiful F-8 Crusader before receiving the F-4B in 1971, the 'Sundowners' accrued more combat experience than any other US Navy fighter squadron during the Vietnam conflict. The last two of the four Phantom II cruises were not technically combat trips as the ceasefire had taken effect in November 1973. However, the squadron still went 'feet dry' in support of the evacuation, as already mentioned (*Bob Archer*)

On long finals to NAF Atsugi (CVW-5's Japanese home near Tokyo), a distinctively coloured VF-151 'Vigilantes' F-4J rips through a typically murky 'Nipponese' sky in February 1978. As with most Phantom II squadrons, VF-151 flew the aircraft for a considerable period of time, 23 years to be exact! Paired with sister-squadron VF-161 'Chargers', VF-151 moved home base from NAS Miramar to NAF Atsugi in the mid 1970s. This aircraft (BuNo 155739) was later converted to S standards as part of the F-4J upgrade programme initiated in the late 1970s (*Masumi Wada via Angelo Romano*)

Considering the age of this venerable old warrior, the fact that this F-4S wears both the Battle Efficient 'E' and the Safety 'S' for sustained operational periods of excellence speaks volumes about the professionalism of VF-151. Seen at rest alongside another ageing warrior of the Vietnam era (a VQ-1 'Bats' EA-3B), this F-4S was enjoying a respite from the action in the calm waters off Fremantle, Western Australia, during CVW-5's last WestPac with the Phantom II

in 1985. One of the major modifications made to the J-models during the upgrade was the introduction of leading-edge slats to the outer wing sections. This gave the F-4 greater manoeuvrability in tight low-speed turns and offered the pilot better control of his mount in the crucial stages just before landing back aboard ship. The port wing slat is clearly visible on this aircraft (*Tony Holmes*)

Although no longer part of the modern US Navy, VF-161 'Chargers' nevertheless flew in the 'frontline' with the F-4 for as long as VF-151, the squadron accounting for no less than six MiGs (including the very last one downed by the Navy in January 1973), during six combat cruises off Vietnam. Wearing the squadron's distinctive black and red tail markings, this 'Chargers' F-4N was photographed in more peaceful times near Atsugi. Flying all four major versions of the naval F-4, the 'Chargers' eventually returned stateside to NAS Lemoore for re-equipment with the F/A-18 Hornet, a process completed by late 1987. Assigned to a new air wing (CVW-10) and redisignated VFA-161 to better reflect their new found attack role, the 'Chargers' carrier qualified with the Hornet and prepared for their first WestPac deployment. However, budget cuts fell upon CVW-10 and the 'Chargers' were forced to disband in April 1988 (*via Angelo Romano*)

Wearing the distinctive Pacific Missile Test Center (PMTC) triangular badge on the tail, an F-4J performs an afterburner departure from homebase, NAS Point Mugu, California. Having carried all manner of ordnance beneath its wings over the years, this Phantom II, and several others in the PMTC fleet, was eventually replaced by the F-14 and F/A-18 in the late 1980s. Because of the nature of their work, the F-4s at Point Mugu were never festooned with the various electronic counter-measures and wing modification kits progressively retrofitted to fleet Phantom IIs, thus, what you see before you is a classically 'stock' St Louis F-4J (*Frank B Mormillo*)

Above Undisputedly the best looking Bicentennial 'bird' of them all, the VX-4 'Evaluators' F-4B is reefed into an eye watering turn over NAS Point Mugu. In fact the scheme was so good VX-4 kept this graphically painted airframe in this condition for sometime after the festivities of 1976 had faded from memory—this photo was taken in November 1977! The 'Evaluators' operated a large fleet of outlandishly coloured F-4s throughout the 1960s and 70s, before finally passing them on to the 'boneyard' at Davis-Monthan AFB in the late 1980s. As their nickname suggests, the squadron was responsible for testing many of the modifications retrofitted to the F-4 during its lifetime. Once they had been safely cleared by VX-4 test pilots the mods went into series production on frontline aircraft (*Frank B Mormillo*)

Left Breaking right into a gap between the clouds over the Californian desert, a pair of F-4Ss from VF-301 'Devil's Disciples' head homeward, bound for NAS Miramar. Both sprayed up in the experimental Heater-Ferris Paint Scheme, the Phantom IIs appear highly visible in this photo. Aimed at breaking up the aircraft's outline, the scheme did not find favour with the Chief of Naval Operations (CNO), disapproving it in May 1984. The final report on the scheme stated, 'It does not appear that the proposed paint scheme would have significant benefits over the current tactical paint scheme when considering all environmental conditions and flight profiles'. VF-301 were the only unit to wear this scheme, and their F-4s were quickly 'greyed out' soon after the CNO findings were released. Now flying the F-14, the reserve-manned 'Disciples' operated the Phantom II for exactly a decade, the aircraft featured in this shot being ex-VF-21 aircraft (*US Navy via David F Brown*)

Above A popular attraction at any airshow it attended, the all-black F-4 became an unofficial trade mark of VX-4. First sprayed up by the squadron in the early 1970s the 'black bunny', or Vandy One as it became known, was just one of several F-4s at Point Mugu camouflaged in a rather unorthodox fashion. Over the years several airframes have worn the prestigious Playboy bunny on their tails, the very first Vandy One being an F-4J, BuNo 153783. Photographed soon after tucking away the gear, this VX-4 crew are strapped into the second Vandy One, F-4S BuNo 158358, which had flown from Point Mugu to Ontario, Canada, for the 1988 London International Airshow. The third Vandy One, F-4S BuNo 158360, recently became the last Phantom II to retire from active Navy service when it left California, bound for Davis-Monthan, in spring 1990 (*Barry Roop via David F Brown*)

Above right Basking in the warm spring sunshine at NAS Patuxent River, this glossy Phantom II was actually the first F-4J built by McDonnell Douglas. Designated McAir Ship 1488 at St Louis, BuNo 153071 was not, however, the first J-model to fly, this honour going to sister-aircraft 153072 at St Louis on 27 May 1966. Both airframes were soon despatched to Pax River to participate in a rigorous flight programme undertaken by the Naval Air Test Center. The J-model Phantom II introduced both structural and avionics upgrades to the Navy F-4. Lower approach speeds to the carrier during landing were achieved by introducing slotted stabilizers and drooped flaps to the tailplane and wings respectively. This lowered the crucial 'over the ramp' speed by almost 12 knots. A beefed-up undercarriage and wider tyres were also fitted beneath the wings, reducing the chances of damage to the aircraft in the result of a heavy landing. Both the radar, the Westinghouse AN/APQ-59, and the fire control system, the AN/AWG-10 (which was also a Westinghouse product) were specially developed for the aircraft, and the twin General Electric J79s were uprated to GE-10 spec, which increased the thrust output of the engines to 17,900 lbs each. Although McDonnell Douglas had

performed a major rework on the Navy Phantom II, the new J-model was cleared for squadron service at Pax River by June 1966, only a month after the first F-4J had flown in Missouri (*Ron McNeil via Angelo Romano*)

Below right Wearing an experimental instrument probe temporarily grafted onto its radome, and the high visibility colours of a test center aircraft on its fin and wingtips, this F-4J/F-4S was captured at rest on the ramp at NAS North Island, California, in October 1976. A very early J-model Phantom II (only the seventh airframe built out of an eventual total of 502 F-4Js delivered), this aircraft never flew with a frontline unit as an F-4S, serving out its time as a hybrid machine at Pax River instead (*Roy Lock via Angelo Romano*)

Above left Although a large aircraft, the F-4J was deemed suitable for close formation work and in due course seven slightly modified airframes were issued to the Blue Angels. Receiving these aircraft was a great boost to the Pensacola, Florida, based team as they had been flying the beautiful, but woefully obsolete, F-11F Tiger for most of the 1960s. Captured on the ramp at RAF Bentwaters in May 1973 during the team's only European tour to date, this F-4J, BuNo 153076, is the sister-aircraft to the Phantom II seen at North Island in the previous photo. Spectacular performers, the F-4Js proved too thirsty for the Carter administration during its post-Vietnam economy drive and the team was forced to trade-in its Phantom IIs for smaller, less JP4-guzzling, A-4F Skyhawks (*Dennis J Calvert*)

Below left An unusual ending for a war-weary airframe. Originally built as an F-4B towards the end of the Bravo model production run in 1965, the aircraft served through the Vietnam conflict, before being chosen as the 214th airframe to be upgraded to N standards in the mid 1970s as part of Project Beeline. Finally grounded in the mid 1980s, the old warrior found a home at NAS Alameda, California, as a deck crew training airframe. This involved the aircraft being shunted around the empty decks of various carriers by greenhorn 'mule' drivers and air wing handlers under the watchful gaze of seasoned flat-top personnel. Somewhere along the line the F-4 has become an honorary member of VFA-131 'Wildcats' – a rather strange honour to be bestowed upon a decidedly grounded aircraft on the west coast of the US by an east coast-based F/A-18 Hornet squadron! (*Angelo Romano*)

Below Unfortunately this is how many F-4s look today. Sprayed in protective latex to seal the airframe up from the elements, this F-4S is devoid of any distinguishing marks – almost. The 'double nuts' OO on the nose wheel door indicates that it was the CO's mount at its final posting. One hopes that the commander, or lieutenant-colonel, who last flew this aircraft wasn't responsible for the rather noticeable dent in the leading edge of the wing (*John Dibbs*)

Marine Machines

When one thinks of F-4s emblazoned with 'stars and bars' the mind conjures up images of powder grey US Navy fighters crammed onto a carrier deck, or row upon row of camouflaged jets at Nellis AFB for a 'Red Flag' exercise. However, one other branch of the US military machine has utilized the Phantom II in large numbers for the past 28 years. The US Marine Corps has equipped 23 squadrons with the F-4 since 1962, although only two reserve units and one frontline reconnaisance squadron are now current with the type.

Part of the F-4 programme right from the start, Marine Corps aviation, just like its pseudo-brethren in the Navy, would be totally transformed with the arrival of the first F-4Bs at MCAS El Toro, California, in May 1962, and at MCAS Beaufort, South Carolina, the following month. Rapidly receiving more Phantom IIs over the next three years, four marine squadrons, under the auspices of Marine Air Group 11 (MAG-11), deployed to Atsugi between 1963 and 1965, before moving on a more permanent basis to Danang, South Vietnam, to help support ground forces during the South-east Asian war. Up until the last F-4 squadron flew its final mission over Vietnam in September 1973, a total of ten Phantom II units had been involved in the conflict. Not only restricted to land bases, one squadron, VMFA-333 'Shamrocks' completed a highly successfully MiG-killing WestPac with CVW-8 aboard USS America (CV-66) in 1972/73.

With the cessation of hostilities, Marine Corps Phantom II squadrons settled down to a less hazardous, but no less demanding, routine of peacetime flying from bases in mainland America, the Pacific and South-east Asia. Occasionally deploying with a carrier air wing into the Atlantic or Western Pacific, 'Corps Phantom II units were rarely spotted back at El Toro or Beaufort for any period of time. One unit that did more than its fair share of travelling was VMFP-3, the sole dedicated Marine Corps reconnaisance squadron flying the unique RF-4B version of the Phantom II. Still soldiering on with the recce F-4 today, VMFP-3 will soon become an RF-18 recce-Hornet unit.

Now all but replaced in USMC service by a more modern McDonnell Douglas strike/fighter, the exploits of the Phantom II have nevertheless earnt the 'bent-winged bird' a special place in 'Flying Leatherneck' history.

'Left a bit, right a bit'. A less than light F-4N from VMFA-323 'Death Rattlers' is carefully winched aboard USS Coral Sea (CV-43) in NAS Alameda dockyard. Along with VMFA-531 'Gray Ghosts', the 'Death Rattlers' created US naval aviation history on this cruise (WestPac 1979/80) by providing total Marine Corps fighter cover for CVW-14. This is the only time in carrier aviation history that a navy air wing has been protected by an all-marine fighter force. The F-4N wears a rainbow coloured rattlesnake on its fin, denoting that BuNo 150480 is in fact the CAG's F-4 in VMFA-323. Re-equipping with the F/A-18A Hornet in 1983, VMFA-323 reacquainted themselves with Coral Sea three years later when they participated in a Med cruise with CVW-13 (Tom Chee via Bob Archer)

Right High over the California desert, three less than pristine VMFA-134 Phantom IIs fly one of the squadron's last sorties with the old F-4S. The only reserve unit at El Toro, VMFA-134 flew the Phantom II for three and a half years before receiving their first F/A-18As in May 1989. The first 'Corps reserve squadron to upgrade to the Hornet, the 'Hawks' have a proud history which dates all the way back to the Pacific in World War 2. Flying TBF/TBM Avengers as VMTB-134, the squadron performed sterling work in the Solomons, at Peleliu and over China before the end of the conflict. Re-activated in 1958 as a reserve fighter squadron, VMF-134 became VMA-134 in 1962 when it received A-4B Skyhawks. The venerable Douglas jet remained in service with the 'Hawks' until the F-4s arrived in 1985 (*Frank B Mormillo*)

Above Loaded up with 500 lb Mk 82 retarded bombs on a TER beneath the starboard wing, and a deadly CBU-59/B Rockeye fragmentation cannister beneath the port wing, this VMFA-134 'Hawks' F-4S should have most 'mud moving' requirements covered with this weapons load. Reposing beneath a typically blue El Toro sky, this rather battered 'Hawks' Phantom II is sprayed up in a typically late-1980s USMC style tactical grey scheme. It would be interesting to know what this aircraft looked like ten years before this photo was taken (*Frank B Mormillo*)

Left Devoid of any distinguishable markings, we will have to take the photographer's word for it when he says that this F-4S belongs to VMFA-232 'Red Devils'. VMFA-232 earned the dubious distinction of being the last American combat unit to leave South-east Asia when it departed from Nam Phong Royal Thai Air Base in August 1974. First seeing action in Vietnam with the F-8E Crusader in the mid 1960s, the 'Red Devils' flew back to the USA to transition onto the F-4J in 1968, before returning to MCAS Iwakuni, Japan. The 1972 Easter invasion of South Vietnam saw the squadron rapidly deploy back into the war zone. Based at the beautiful air station at Kaneohe Bay, Hawaii, for over a decade now, VMFA-232 traded in their F-4s for brand new F/A-18Cs in early 1989. The three external tanks mounted beneath this aircaft suggest that it is returning from a transpac deployment stateside (*Frank B Mormillo*)

Above A little more colourful than the previous 'Red Devils' F-4S, this grubby F-4J, photographed in the pattern at NAF Atsugi in November 1978, hardly makes up for the former glory days of the squadron early on in the decade though. Some miles from Kaneohe Bay, the crew of this Phantom II have bolted on the essential travel tank to the inboard starboard pylon. Soon to be returned to the Naval Air Rework Facility (NARF) at NAS North Island for updating to F-4S specs, this weary jet (BuNo 155801) was the sister-ship to the most famous F-4J of them all, BuNo 155800. Better known as SHOWTIME 100 of VF-96 'Fighting Falcons', this aircraft, crewed by Lieutenant Randy Cunningham and Lieutenant jg (junior grade) Willie Driscoll, shot down three MiG-17s in one engagement on 10 May 1972, before being knocked down by a SAM-2 surface-to-air missile. Cunningham and Driscoll, with two MiG kills to their credit already, became the only Navy aces of the war as a result of their success during this mission (*Masumi Wada via Angelo Romano*)

Right All aircraft eventually reach the end of their careers but unfortunately some do not get to retire gracefully. Sitting side by side on the Kaneohe fire dump, this forlorn pair of F-4Ss from VMFA-232 have only each other for company. However, I'm sure if they could talk they would rivet many an aviation buff to the spot! Judging by the fact that both aircraft have similar panels missing, it can be assumed that the maintenance shop at VMFA-232 began to run short of suitable spares towards the end of the Phantom II's time at Kaneohe

Above The most formidable pilot/RIO pairing in MAG-24 (Kaneohe's controlling body) (*Both photos by Steve Mansfield*)

Left Similarly battered F-4S, different fire dump. Lying motionless behind the rework hangar at MCAS Cherry Point, North Carolina, this Phantom II has seen many a practice crew extraction inflicted upon it, as the jagged metal around the cockpit clearly shows. Although totally gutted, the abundance of 'plumbing' within the nose of this F-4 gives you some idea of how complex an aircraft the Phantom II was beneath the skin (*Steve Mansfield*)

Above Gear locked down, flaps and leading edge slats deployed, the CO of VMFA-122 'Crusaders' approaches the vast expanse of Kadena AFB after completing a practice bombing sortie off Okinawa. Like VMFA-232, the commencement of hostilities in Vietnam had seen VMFA-122 equipped with the F-8 Crusader. Indeed, the squadron had been the first unit in the 'Corps to receive this sleek fighter from Vought, hence their nickname from 1957 onwards (*Masumi Wada via Angelo Romano*)

Above left Parked at the 'last chance' checkpoint, this pair of lightly loaded F-4Js prepare for another bombing sortie during the 1978 WestPac det to Kadena from homebase at MCAS Beaufort. The small blue sword on the fin of each aircraft is a marking which has adorned VMFA-122 machines since the late 1950s. Transitioning onto the F-4B in the mid 1960s, the 'Crusaders' were soon in the thick of things in Vietnam, deploying to Danang in 1967 for a 12 month tour. The squadron eventually traded in their F-4s 19 years later for F/A-18As, thus making them the second east coast unit to re-equip with the Hornet (*Masumi Wada via Angelo Romano*)

Below Left More MAG-24 Kaneohe-based Phantom IIs. These two F-4Js belong to VMFA-212 'Lancers', and are seen departing Kadena for the Hawaiian islands on 16 September 1978. Photographed during a time of great change colour wise for 'Corps squadrons, VMFA-212's embracing of the new directives can be seen to vary from aircraft to aircraft—notice the two styles of national insignia. One thing's for sure though, the 'Lancers' would definitely win the award for the most dire tail markings seen in this period. Unlike many USMC F-4 units, VMFA-212 was spared the brutality of a war cruise over the skies of Vietnam. As with sister-squadron VMFA-232, the 'Lancers' are now fully operational with the F/A-18C (*Masumi Wada via Angelo Romano*)

Above Back to the halcyon days of Marine Corps colours, this July 1976 shot of a VMFA-312 'Checkertails' F-4J at MCAS Beaufort shows just how outrageous some squadron markings became. When first equipped with F-4Bs in the early 1960s, VMFA-312 had adorned their aircraft with a subtle band of checkers across the fin of their aircraft. However, over the next ten years the remainder of the fin was slowly painted in squadron colours until finally there was no room left and the paint shop started an assault on the fuselage as well! Appropriately, during the Bicentennial year VMFA-312 have suitably modified the colours of their squadron titling to reflect their patriotic feelings. Surprisingly, the F-4 behind this moving 'canvas' is devoid of any squadron markings – perhaps the paint shop ran out of VMFA-312 colours! Like all other Beaufort-based F-4 units of the 1970s and 80s, the 'Checkertails' now fly more sedately 'markinged' F/A-18s (*Kenneth W Buchanan via Angelo Romano*)

Left Besides VMFA-112 'Wolf Pack' who are based in Dallas, Texas, the only other flyers of the F-4S are these guys, VMFA-321 'Hells Angels', based at Andrews AFB, Washington DC. A reservist unit who previously flew the F-8 Crusader, the 'Angels' received their first F-4Bs in late 1973, progressively updating to the N- and finally to the S-model in 1985. Once a very colourful squadron who would liberally daub the entire fin and spine of their aircraft in bright blue paint, and then 'sprinkle' stars over the finished job for good measure, the 'Angels' now wear a more subdued finish. The navy blue patches on the radome, spine and wings of this F-4 do add some interest to the dreaded tactical paint scheme (TPS) however. A very early production F-4J, this particular Phantom II (BuNo 153887) was also one of the first J-models pulled from service and upgraded to S-specs. Awaiting its crew on a fine June morning, and plugged into the mobile generator to provide power for the internal systems before engine fire up, this aircraft proudly wears the 'double nuts' 'OO' modex beneath the cockpit, thus denoting it as being the CO's personal Phantom II (*Robbie Shaw*)

Below Under assault by squadron armourers, this smart F-4J belonged to MiG-killing VMFA-333 'Shamrocks' and was attached to CVW-8 for the inaugural cruise of USS *Nimitz* (CVN-68) to the Med in 1976. The only Marine Corps squadron to embark with an air wing on a combat cruise to Vietnam, the 'Shamrocks' performed admirably whilst aboard the USS *America* (CV-66) during the vessel's 158 days on the line in 1972/73. Completing many bombing sorties during *Linebacker* operations over North Vietnam, the 'Shamrocks' also managed to bag the only all-Marine MiG kill of the war on 11 September 1972. Flying F-4J BuNo 155526, call sign SHAMROCK 201, Major Lee 'Bear' Lasseter and Captain John Cummings downed a MiG-21 with an AIM-9G Sidewinder. However, five minutes after claiming the MiG, they too were hit by a SAM as they crossed the coast on their way back to the carrier. Both men were subsequently rescued by a US Navy helicopter. Including SHAMROCK 201, VMFA-333 lost a total of three F-4Js during the cruise. This particular aircraft has its radome open revealing the dish of the APQ-59 radar system, and an inflight refuelling probe is also visible in the extended position. Although the 'Shamrocks' continued to fly the F-4 until re-equipping with the Hornet in 1987, no more carrier cruises have been undertaken by the squadron since the *Nimitz* trip (*Angelo Romano*)

Heading for California, a trio of VMFP-3 'Specters', (or 'The Eyes of the Corps' depending on your preference), RF-4B Phantom IIs prepare to roll down Kaneohe Bay's short runway. Stopping over at 'K-Bay' during a TransPac from Iwakuni back to homebase at El Toro, this trio of RF-4s had just completed their regular six-month long detachment to the Japanese island base in support of MAG-12. As flight leader, the pilot in the RF-4B on the right has deployed the leading edge wing slats in preparation for his imminent departure from K-Bay. Being thirsty jets, all three RF-4s have the mandatory trio of external tanks bolted beneath them, this extra fuel capacity helping to quench the twin J79's demand for JP4 (*Steven Mansfield*)

Right Looking a million dollars, this dazzling Phantom II was photographed on the Andrews ramp in April 1988. The squadron has cleverly incorporated the Air Force-style formation strip light on the fin into its tail design. The glossy finish of the paint on this F-4S is also rather unusual, the aircraft hardly looking 21-plus years old. VMFA-321 are scheduled to receive F/A-18s in fiscal year 1992 (*David F Brown*)

Above A resting home for many old
warriors, the NARF at North Island is
littered with several RF-4 'shells'. The fifth
recce-Phantom II to roll off the production
line at St Louis, this knackered airframe had
already spent six years out in the open at
North Island when this photo was taken in
August 1988. Just discernable on the spine
are the faded words 'USS *Midway*', denoting
that this ex-VMFP-3 RF-4 participated in the
squadron's last deployment on a WestPac
cruise with CVW-5 in 1981. As with most
struck-off RF-4s, this airframe has been
cannibalized of any useable parts to keep
fellow recce-Phantom IIs operable at El
Toro (*John Dibbs*)

Above Refuelling probes at 'the salute,' four recce-Phantom IIs rest on the Kaneohe transient ramp before pressing on to El Toro. The window just in front of the air conditioning intake usually houses a lateral KS-87 large format camera, although the 'see through' aspect of this RF-4B suggests that the slender nose of this aircraft is 'cameraless'. The squadron only has about 20 RF-4s on strength now as many have been retired due to their lack of remaining airframe hours (*Steve Mansfield*)

Right Stripped back to bare metal, the tailcone reveals some interesting details. Starting from immediately above the cone, the T-shaped device is the jettison pipe for the main fuselage fuel cell. The pair of 'eyes' just below that are antennae for the radar warning receiver (RWR) kit fitted to the F-4. A vital system which warns the crew that they are being tracked by unfriendly radar, the small domes cover spiral helix receivers which, together with the wingtip RWRs, give the Phantom II 360° cover. The D-shaped 'mouth' beneath the RWR bulges serves as a 'peep hole' for groundcrew to check that the parabrake chute has been installed correctly. When the pilot chooses to deploy the parachute, the tailcone hinges upwards and the large chute streams out (*Steve Mansfield*)

The 'All-Service' Fighter

For many years an intense rivalry has existed between the US Air Force and the Navy over combat aircraft, and the roles they should perform. Only twice in their history have both silver- and gold-winged pilots flown similar hardware; in the early 1950s the Navy operated the FJ Fury from its carriers. Basically an uprated and navalized F-86 Sabre, the Fury was developed as a stop-gap measure whilst the Navy waited for a suitably powerful fighter of its own to fly from its fleet of 'flat tops'. One of the aircraft under development at that stage would eventually fly with many of those squadrons equipped with the Fury, but more importantly would find favour with the Air Force and basically revolutionize their methods of waging war. That aircraft was, of course, the F-4 Phantom II.

Flown head-to-head in 1961 with the Air Force's super fighter of the time, the F-106 Delta Dart, during Project HIGHSPEED, the Phantom II clearly emerged as the superior aircraft both in the air and on the ground. A true multi-role machine the likes of which the USAF had never seen before, the F-4 appealed not only because it could perform the fighter role clinically well, but also because it could deliver a large payload of ordnance at extreme range with virtually pin-point accuracy on the same sortie! The top brass had to admit that the Navy had got it very right; so right in fact that the Air Force would eventually operate close on to 3000 Phantom IIs in five different versions. Responsible for drastically upgrading the basic aircraft over the years, the USAF has issued the F-4 to the Tactical Air Command (TAC), Air National Guard (ANG), Air Force Reserve and Air Force Systems Command. With over 1000 still in frontline service today, the F-4 is far from being a spent force with the modern USAF.

Besides operating the aircraft as a straight fighter/bomber, the Air Force also developed the F-4 to fulfil the reconnaisance role, 503 RF-4Cs eventually joining the TAC ranks. Later on in its life, the ultimate Phantom II, the F-4E, was converted into a radar hunting, SAM-busting, 'Wild Weasel', 116 of these extremely potent aircraft being issued to TAC squadrons.

The legendary USAF aircraft of the Vietnam conflict, the 'de-navalized' F-4 has earned for itself a formidable reputation over the past 28 years. The fighter of the sixties and seventies, the Phantom II was far from overshadowed in USAF service in the eighties, and will undoubtedly press on into the nineties and beyond.

Tanking completed (note the JP4 smears behind the refuelling receptacle), another 163rd TFS F-4C drops behind the KC-135 before diving away into the cloud below. Like many 'Guard units in the 1970s, the 163rd flew the stylish F-100D Super Sabre until the first F-4C arrived at Fort Wayne Municipal Airport, Indiana, in late 1979. Still plugging away with the F-4 today, the squadron now flies the more capable E-model Phantom II (*Frank B Mormillo*)

Left Another unit familiar with European skies operated this particular F-4C. The 163rd TFS, Indiana ANG, deployed with their F-84F Thunderstreaks to Chambley AB, France, during the Berlin Crisis of 1961, returning to Indiana in August 1962. Twenty-three years later, and high above the parched desert of Arizona, an F-4C with refuelling receptable agape slowing closes on a SAC KC-135 after completing a practice bombing mission over the Nellis AFB ranges. Wearing the dark greens synonymous with the then fashionable 'Europe One' or 'Lizard' camouflage scheme, the squadron has at least kept a splash of 163rd TFS red on the tip of each drop tank (*Frank B Mormillo*)

Above Another long term F-101 user, but on the other side of the country, the 136th FIS, New York ANG, also received the F-4C in 1982. Part of the 107th FIG (in fact the only squadron in the 107th FIG!), the boys from Niagara Falls International Airport are still flying the trusty old F-4, although in the slightly more updated form of the Delta model (*David F Brown*)

Below Now only to be found in dwindling numbers on the vast ramps at Edwards AFB, the original Air Force Phantom II, the F-4C, spent its final days performing sterling work with the 'weekend warriors' of the Air National Guard. First assigned to the 170th Tactical Fighter Squadron (TFS), Illinois ANG, in January 1972, the F-4C later went on to serve with no less than 16 'Guard squadrons, including the 114th Tactical Fighter Training Squadron (TFTS) of the Oregon ANG whose Phantom IIs are pictured here high over the Mojave Desert in September 1988. Each wearing a telemetry pod on their starboard Sidewinder rails, this 'lose duece' are shaping up to tank from a Strategic Air Command (SAC) KC-135 during a break in *Lobo Flag*, a 'Guard sponsored tactical fighter exercise. Part of the 142nd Fighter Interceptor Group (FIG), the 112th formed in the mid eighties as the sole training unit for ANG F-4C pilots and weapons system operators (WSO). Now an F-16A Air Defence Fighting Falcon unit, the 112th is currently in the process of working up with the General Dynamics fighter at their homebase of Kingsley Field, Oregon (*Frank B Mormillo*)

Right The other F-4C squadron in the Oregon ANG was the 123rd FIS, a seasoned fighter unit which had flown everything from F-51 Mustangs through to F-101 Voodoos since the late 1940s. Trading in their venerable McDonnell F-101s in 1982, the squadron received another St Louis product, in the form of the Phantom II, soon afterwards. Also photographed during *Lobo Flag*, this decidedly matt grey F-4 is being carefully manoeuvred towards the tanker's boom, the pilot having already opened the refuelling receptacle door on the spine of the aircraft. Interestingly, the 123rd did not receive the F-16 like their fellow Oregon ANG brothers. Instead, 20 F-15A Eagles now sit on the squadron ramp at Portland International Airport (*Frank B Mormillo*)

Above A long way from home, this line up of 184th TFS, Arkansas ANG, F-4Cs had deployed across the Atlantic to Eskisehir Air Base, Turkey, in September 1986 for the annual NATO *Display Determination* exercise. Displaying their own style of determination, the Arkansas boys had their hands full keeping their weary jets serviceable in the heat of the Turkish summer. Part of the ANG *Coronet Cherokee* deployment for that year, the arrival of the F-4Cs added further flavour to the mix of aircraft participating in the huge exercise. Each of these aircraft carry practice bombs beneath the Sidewinder rails, this ordnance no doubt being dropped on the extensive weapons ranges in Turkey. Having received their first F-4Cs in 1979, the 184th made full use of their aircraft before finally retiring them to Davis-Monthan in 1987. Based at Fort Smith Municipal Airport (Ebing ANGB), the squadron now flies F-16s (*Yves Debay*)

Right Harking back ten years to the colourful 'glory days' of the F-4C and the ANG, this 113th TFS Phantom II is temporarily parked on one of the taxiways at RAF Alconbury while a 'groundie' scurries about under the forward gear well, trying to find the source of the pilot's problem. Having just completed an Atlantic crossing from deepest Indiana to the dampness of Cambridgeshire, this F-4C looks resplendent in its South-east Asian camouflage. The second Phantom II squadron in the Indiana ANG, the 113th FIS comes under the control of the 181st TFG; unlike the 163rd who answer to the 122nd TFW. Also a former F-100 squadron, the 113th received its F-4s at about the same time as the 163rd (*Robbie Shaw*)

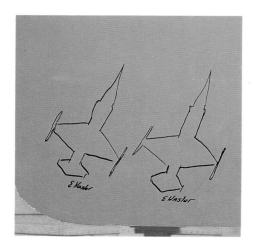

Above Up against an F-15 or F-16, the F-4 pilot had his work cut out for him. However, go head-to-head with a point-and-shoot interceptor like the F-104G Starfighter and the Air Guard jock should have come out the victor every time. Just to prove a point, this 'cocky' 184th TFS pilot has 'bagged' two Turkish Starfighters during the deployment (*Yves Debay*)

Left 'Flying' between the hangars at RAF Upper Heyford during the base open house in May 1990, this decidedly slate grey F-4C once belonged to the 182nd TFS, Texas ANG, at Kelly AFB. Resident at 'Heyford for the past four years as the base battle damage repair airframe, the Phantom II wore full ANG livery for some time before being unceremoniously resprayed in this rather unattractive scheme. The bulge under the radome is a legacy of the F-4B, the naval fighter carrying an infra-red tracking probe immediately beneath the radar dish to aid in target acquisition. The Air Force saw no need for this device and deleted it from the finished F-4C. However, such was the demand for the Phantom II that the Air Force refrained from asking McDonnell Douglas to recontour the radome, thus allowing the flow of both F-4Bs and Cs to roll down the St Louis production line unabated (*Anthony Thornborough*)

Above The 'Happy Hooligans' of the 178th FIS, North Dakota ANG, have worn some rather lurid schemes over the years on aircraft like the F-102 Delta Dagger and the F-101 Voodoo. However, none have been quite so outlandish as this one on F-4D 66-498, which was resprayed to celebrate North Dakota's admission to the Union of the United States. The large circular logo, which consists of a stem of wheat and a pioneer family, was the official North Dakota motif for the celebrations in 1989. Although not visible in this shot, a large state seal was also sprayed onto the underside of the F-4. Part of the 119th FIG based at Hector Field, Fargo, the 'Happy Hooligans', like most other ANG fighter units, enjoy a proud history with fast jets that stretches back to the F-94 Starfire, the first of which arrived in North Dakota in June 1954. Arguably the most experienced F-4D operators in the world today, the 178th received their first Phantom IIs in March 1977 (*Gary Meinert via Robbie Shaw*)

An historical gathering of 'iron eagles', or should it be Kansas ANG 'Jayhawks'? Flying high over the New Mexico desert, formating off the starboard wing of a 134th Air Refuelling Group, Tennessee ANG, KC-135E, these four 184th TFG F-4Ds are about to refuel for the last time during their journey down to the 'boneyard' at Davis-Monthan AFB. A haven for F-4Ds, both squadrons within the 184th shared up to 54 Big Uglies, these aircraft flying many hours with trainee crews at the controls. Equipping the 127th and the 161st TFTS, both units flew the venerable F-4D from the ANG side of McConnell AFB, a huge SAC facility in the heart of Kansas
(*David F Brown*)

Above Viewed through the 'boomers' window in the KC-135, 66-759 pulls back from the tanker before joining the formation off the starboard wingtip. Like most of the other 'Jayhawk' F-4s, this aircraft earned its 'military medal' over Vietnam in the late 1960s. A training group since its days with the mighty F-105 Thunderchief, the 184th graduated over 1220 pilots and WSOs during its 11-year association with the F-4. Regularly flying over 9600 training sorties annually, the 'Jayhawks' have accrued more F-4D hours than any other group in the Air Force. Not only responsible for instructing ANG crews, the 184th have also trained their fair share of reserve and active service pilots and WSOs. As well as introducing ab initio aviators to the intricacies of the Phantom II, the 184th also ran the F-4 Fighter Weapons School until 1988. A direct counterpart of the Navy's Fighter Weapons School (Top Gun) at Miramar, the group devised its own demanding syllabus which honed the edge of Phantom II crews to razor sharpness. Still training ANG fighter pilots today, the 184th now has a large complement of F-16 Fighting Falcons (*David F Brown*)

Right Coming in for a close look at the tanker, the pilot stares up out of the cockpit of his F-4 and straight at the refuelling probe. Maintaining station at this height, the Phantom II driver will now wait for the 'boomer' aboard the KC-135 to fly the refuelling probe into the gaping receptable in the middle of the fuselage spine (*David F Brown*)

Above left Not all the F-4Ds supplied to the 'Guard have been operated in the dual fighter/bomber role, as evidenced by this beautiful air superiority grey machine from the 179th Fighter Interceptor Squadron (FIS), Minnesota ANG. Although in the minority when compared to 'mud moving' TFSs, interceptor units have nevertheless given both the 'Guard and the regular Air Force sterling service over the past 15 years. Helping out the USAFE in this instance, the Minnesota ANG was one of several 'Guard FISs that in 1986 fulfilled the vital alert duty at Ramstein AB, Germany, whilst the resident frontline unit, the 86th TFW, was back in the USA converting from the F-4E to the F-16C. Armed with live AIM-9J Sidewinders on the inboard wing pylons, and a quartet of fuselage mounted AIM-7F Sparrows, this F-4C is hooked up to the power cart ready for a 'Zulu' launch should the need arise. Interestingly, somewhere along the line the boys from Duluth have souvenired an Oregon ANG 142nd FIG belly tank, the offending item skulking beneath the fuselage of this aircraft (*Robert Marx via Robbie Shaw*)

Below left They don't come prettier than this 171st FIS, Michigan ANG, Phantom II photographed at McConnell in April 1990 during the 'Phantom Pharewell' weekend which saw the Kansas ANG say goodbye to their F-4Ds. One of four Phantom IIs that trekked down to Kansas from Selfridge ANGB (behind this aircraft is a 'clone' all-grey F-4D), this Phantom II has been on the squadron books since the mid 1980s. Initially receiving F-4Cs as F-106 replacements in 1978, the 171st should eventually receive the specially modified air defence version of the F-16A. Like all other ANG interceptor units, the squadron has toned down its Phantom IIs over the past two to three years, most aircraft now wearing the matt 'Egypt One' tactical grey scheme (*Steve Hill*)

Above Landing light ablaze, a well-used F-4E of the 526th TFS is lined up for a routine landing at Aviano AB in Italy. A late-production F-4E, this aircraft had nevertheless seen a hard decade's service with the 86th TFW by the time this photo was taken in February 1981, and would remain on strength with the wing until flown back to the USA in 1986. Obviously planning on being away from German skies for some time, the crew have ensured that a travel pod has been bolted between the belly and the starboard external tanks. Tactically minded right down to the last detail, the squadron have even camouflaged this 'luxury' store! (*Bob Archer*)

Making a practice approach at the boom, an early-production F-4E, carrying the distinctive 'RS' tail code of Ramstein AB on its tail, cruises over the calm waters of the Mediterranean in November 1976. Wearing red 'boot topping' on its fin, this F-4 belongs to the 'Black Knights' of the 526th TFS, which, along with the 512th TFS, have constituted the 86th TFW for over 25 years. Based at Ramstein since January 1973, the 86th initially flew the F-4C before transitioning on to the more versatile E-model in the mid seventies. Like most former Phantom II wings, the 86th now fly the F-16C in large numbers (*Angelo Romano*)

Right For many years an F-4 operator, the 4th TFW at Seymour Johnson AFB is currently in the process of transitioning from the Phantom II to the formidable F-15E Strike Eagle. Looking resplendent in its 'Egypt One' greys, a remarkably clean F-4E from the 334th 'Eagles' TFS slowly closes on the KC-10 Extender that will pump it full of JP4 (*Mark Wagner*)

Below The 4th TFW consists of three squadrons—the 334th, 335th and 336th TFSs, who up until 1989, had flown the F-4E for almost 20 years. The first squadron to say goodbye to the Phantom II was the 336th TFS, nicknamed 'The Rockets', two of their former mounts being photographed here in formation over the Atlantic en route to Europe. Distinguished by their yellow fin caps (the other two units wearing blue and green respectively), these aircraft both wear specially marked travel pods on the inner port wing pylons. Also readily apparent is the amount of stencilling all over the aircraft, these vital marks telling the groundcrew what exterior panel covers what. Turning the F-4 into a 'flying technical manual', the stencilling helped ease the groundcrews' headaches when it came to fixing the jet (*Denis J Calvert*)

Above Wearing a 'slightly' unusual paint scheme an anonymous F-4E taxies out for a test flight at Bergstrom AFB, Texas. Home to a large population of RF-4Cs, Bergstrom is also the site of a large rework depot which specializes in major overhauls of Phantom IIs. Devoid of any distinguishing marks, including a serial number, this F-4 has been liberally coated in zinc chromate primer, a non-corrosive base colour used on all military aircraft. The radome has been left alone, however, as this will be coated in its own special rubberized paint once the flight tests have been satisfactorily completed (*David F Brown*)

You can just hear the groundcrew saying to themselves 'dang, it's hot and noisy out here!' Engines on idle, cockpits cranked and hands resting on the canopy framing, the ambient temperature is steadily rising at ramp level as this 4th TFW Phantom II is given the final once over before being sent on its way to drop practice bombs somewhere in North Carolina. Representing the ultimate F-4 in USAF service, this final-batch Phantom II has all the trick modifications fitted to it in various excrescences on its wings and fuselage. Starting with the nose, the fairing for the M61A1 20 mm cannon, unique to the F-4E, has been extended to house the longer barrelled, uprated version of the venerable weapon. Immediately to the right of the black cannon fairing is an ALQ-131 noise and deception electronic counter measures pod, a vital 'bolt-on extra' which has greatly enhanced the F-4's survivability. Lastly, just above the port TER is the Target Identification System Electro-Optical (TISEO) device, this spherical fairing containing a telescopic camera which is slaved to a TV receiver in the WSO's 'rear office'. Linked to the large number of laser-guided and electro-optical weapons that appeared as a result of lessons learned in Vietnam in the early 1970s, the TISEO system is one of the more distinguishing features of the late-production F-4E (*Mark Wagner*)

Above The state of New Jersey has two fast jet squadrons within its borders, one flying the F-16 in the fighter interceptor role (119th FIS) at Atlantic City, and the other assigned the tactical strike mission with the F-4E (141st TFS) at McGuire AFB. Soon to receive the ubiquitous F-16, the 141st have been Phantom II-equipped since the first D-models arrived at McGuire in 1981. As with all squadron aircraft, this shabby F-4E wears a charging tiger motif on the nose and 'New Jersey' titling, in an orange strip, on the fin (*Tim Laming*)

Above right The 110th TFS, Missouri ANG, have come a long way since they first flew the Curtiss JN-4 Jenny biplane back in June 1923. One thing hasn't changed in all that time though—the squadron is still based at Lambert Field, St Louis. One of the oldest ANG squadrons in existence today, the unit started life as the 110th Observation Squadron, a role they continued to perform right through the thirties and into World War 2. Flying an assortment of equipment after 1945, the 110th TFS eventually received the F-4C in early 1979. Having now progressed to the E-model, the squadron continues to disturb the peace at Lambert Field with their thundering afterburner take-offs. Less than a mile from its birthplace, this Phantom II is truly at 'home' in St Louis (*Steve Hill*)

Below right Only two Air Force Reserve (AFRES) squadrons fly the Phantom II, and both are based in the 'Lone Star' state of Texas. Slated for conversion onto the F-16, the F-4E-equipped units have, in the meantime, been experimenting with unorthodox camouflage schemes, as witnessed by this 704th TFS aircraft departing on a bombing mission during the annual *Gunsmoke* exercise at Nellis. Carrying a pair of Mk 82 500 lb 'iron' bombs on the inboard pylon and a data pod on the Sidewinder rail, this AFRES machine has been liberally daubed with a slightly glossy Prussian blue shade over its more standard light grey base scheme. Built 17 years ago, this aircraft is one of the newer F-4Es in the Air Force fleet and was photographed soon after departure from Nellis in October 1989 (*David F Brown*)

Below Just as the Navy/Marines had their rare version of the Phantom II (the RF-4B), so too did the Air Force. Although not exactly new-build F-4s, 116 E-models were modified enough to warrant a designation change into the F-4G Wild Weasel, a dedicated radar killer if ever there was one. Filled with highly sensitive radar homing and warning devices, and festooned with no fewer than 52 extra aerials, the F-4G was developed to perform one task, and one task only. Equipping only a handful of crack fighter squadrons, most Wild Weasel Phantom IIs are to be found at George AFB, California, a west coast haven for F-4s. This particular Wild Weasel was photographed

over Arizona soon after refuelling from a KC-135. Taking part in a *Red Flag* sortie, it is devoid of external stores except for a dummy Texas Instruments AGM-88A High-speed Anti-Radiation Missile (HARM). Flown on this occasion by the now defunct 563rd TFS, the aircraft was at the time controlled by the 37th TFW. However, the former George AFB wing is now based at Tonopah Air Force Station, Nevada, flying the stealthy F-117A 'Nighthawk'. The 561st TFS and 562nd TFTS, formerly part of the 37th TFW, are still F-4E/G-equipped though and are now controlled by the biggest Phantom II group in the USAF, the 35th TFG (*Frank B. Mormillo*)

Right The result of bitter lessons learnt in Vietnam and the Middle East, the F-4G was built as an answer to the deadly SAM, its main armament, the 'smart' AGM-88, being able to sniff out a missile site at great distances. The heart of the aircraft is the McDonnell Douglas AN/APR-38 radar and missile detection and launch homing system, much of this kit being fitted in the former cannon fairing beneath the radome. This F-4G, trailing the boom high over the Atlantic, wears the early delivery scheme of the Wild Weasel—South-east Asian brown, green and tan, Belonging to the 52nd TFW at Spangdahlem in Germany, this aircraft has worn two other styles of camouflage since this shot was taken in October 1981 (*Tim Laming*)

EJECTION SEAT
AND
CANOPY

U.S. AIR FORCE F4G
A.F. SERIAL NO. 69
SERVICE THIS AIRCR
WITH GRADE JP-4 FU
IDENTIPLATE LOCATI

Left Sitting on a mass of tubes, wiring and seat-shaped steel, strapped into the ultimate hot-rod, the fighter pilot and the Phantom II have been inseparable for the past 30 years. Enjoying the view from their lofty perch, this 52nd TFW pilot and WSO wait while a fellow Spangdahlem crew complete preflights in the aircraft behind them (*Ian Black*)

Below Six years later 'fashionable' 52nd TFW F-4Gs were wearing the wrap-around 'lizard' scheme. Spied on a grey day at RAF Mildenhall, this F-4G even has its own personal 'six-shooter' to increase its firepower. Although suffering from the 'Europe One' disease that afflicted most USAFE units in the mid eighties, at least this aircraft has a low-viz shark's mouth on its forward fuselage (with a very large red tongue!). The front of the AN/ALQ-131(V) ECM pod is also clearly visible strapped to the fuselage of this F-4G (*Ian Black*)

The lastest scheme worn by F-4Gs in Europe is beautifully illustrated by this shot of an 81st TFS/52nd TFW Wild Weasel climbing out of Upper Heyford in May 1990. Three units share 40 F-4Gs at Spangdahlem, each one marking its own aircraft with a stripe on the fin tip. Besides the 81st, the 23rd (blue) and 480th (red) TFSs can be found at 'Spang'. Like US-based Wild Weasel wings, the 52nd originally flew both the E- and G-model Phantom II before retiring its Echoes in 1987 and receiving the F-16C in return. With the F-4G as the 'hunter' and the F-16C as the 'killer', the 52nd has a formidable anti-radar/anti-missile capability (*Paul Cabby*)

A familiar sight in British skies for almost 22 years, the 'AR' coded RF-4Cs of the 10th Tactical Reconnaissance Wing (TRW) arrived at RAF Alconbury on 12 May 1965, commencing a working relationship with the base that was to last until April 1987. Originally a three squadron wing, the 10th only controlled the 1st TRS by the time it came to shut up shop in the UK. Also now defunct is this particular RF-4C, the current Air Force listings not showing it as being on strength with any recce unit. Besides the white in the 'star and bar' fuselage insignia, only the crews' bonedomes serve to brighten up this drab Phantom II, photographed as it departed on a sortie from Alconbury in March 1982 (*Robbie Shaw*)

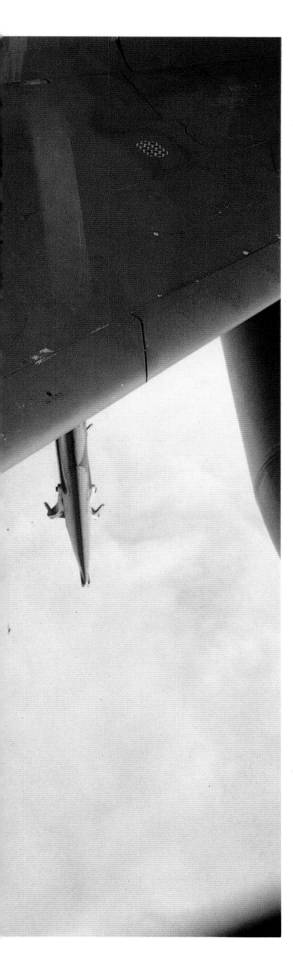

Left With his WSO head-down in the rear-seat, the pilot keeps his eyes firmly planted on the 'Christmas tree' lights on the underside of the tanker. As soon as he sees a red he knows the boomer will soon be disengaging. Flying, rather appropriately, under the call sign of XEROX ONE, this well-worn RF-4 hails from Zweibrucken in Germany. Since the 10th TRW was disbanded in 1987 only 23 RF-4Cs remain in Europe, all assigned to the 38th TFS/26th TRW. At first glance this may seem a small number, but remember the Luftwaffe fly the survivors of 88 RF-4Es delivered to them in the early 1970s, these aircraft combined giving NATO a more than competent recce force. Slated for closure under planned Air Force cuts in 1993, the future of Zweibrucken, and the 26th TRW, does not look entirely rosy (*Tim Laming*)

Above Although USAFE colour schemes were supposed to be purged of colour by the mid 1980s, someone forgot to tell the 1st TRS. Wearing a stylish fin cap decoration and snappy drop shadow tail codes, this RF-4C is about to complete the short hop from RAF Alconbury to RAF Mildenhall to participate in the 10th TRW's last Air Fete. The crew have even brought along a special customized travel pod, full, no doubt, with 10th TRW patches, zaps and coffee mugs to sell to the British public (*Mike Vines—Photo Link*)

Left A major operator of the standard F-4 over the years, the ANG also equipped many of its squadrons with the recce Phantom II. In fact, the 'Guard received RF-4Cs almost 12 months before it saw C-model Phantom IIs, the first recce squadron being issued with aircraft in February 1971. Signalling a major upgrading in 'Guard capabilities, the honour of being the inaugural RF-4 unit went to the 'good old boys' of the 106th TRS, Alabama ANG, who are still flying the aircraft today! This RF-4,

however, hails from 'potato country', belonging to the 190th TRS, Idaho ANG. Wearing drab 'Europe One' colours and devoid of any distinguishing marks, it has just finished refuelling from a KC-135. Also part of the 190th TRS is the 189th Tactical Reconnaissance Training Flight (TRTF), who, since 1983, have been responsible for training all ANG RF-4 pilots and WSOs. Both units are based at Boise Municipal Airport (*David Donald*)

Below Probably the last unit to form on the RF-4C, the 196th TFS, California ANG, is currently trading in their weary F-4Es for positively geriatric recce Phantom IIs. Although at least 20 years old, the lead RF-4 in this line-up seems to be coping with old age rather well. Flown hard and fast at low level throughout their respective careers, the majority of the airframes now in service with the 196th were amongst the initial batch of RF-4s delivered to the Air Force way back in 1964/65. This makes them the oldest Phantom IIs in service anywhere in the world (*Tim Laming*)

Not exactly on long finals, the pilot of this RF-4 has selected gear down purely for the benefit of the camera. Wearing the distinctive Shogun's head on the intake, this aircraft could only belong to one squadron, the formerly Kadena-based 15th TRS. The only dedicated photographic unit in the Pacific Air Forces, the 15th have operated the recce-Phantom II since 1967, receiving a brand new batch of 24 RF-4Cs to replace their battle-weary RF-101 Voodoos. During 1990 the squadron left Okinawa after 34 years and moved to Taegu AB, South Korea, passing from the 18th TFW to the 51st TFW in the process. However, their stay in South Korea promises to be only a brief one—the 15th TRS is due for deactivation in 1991 (*Peter R Foster*)

Flying at a more sedate pace nowadays, the 165th TRS, Kentucky ANG, has, since 1989, been a TAS (Tactical Airlift Squadron) equipped with the obsolescent C-130B Hercules. Harking back to when Kentucky ANG aircraft had only two engines and two crew, this sharp-looking RF-4 idles on the Alconbury ramp during *Best Focus* 1982, an annual recce event held by the 10th TRW for both active and ANG squadrons. Although most of the 165th's RF-4s went to the burgeoning 190th TRS in Idaho, this particular aircraft has disappeared from the listings, possibly depatched to Davis-Monthan dues to its lack of airframe hours (*Robbie Shaw*)

Where would a chapter on the USAF/ANG Phantom II be without a photo of these guys, the 'good old boys' from Alabama. Already a highly seasoned reconnaissance unit when the first RF-4s arrived at Birmingham Muncipal Airport in 1971, the 106th TRS has gone on to establish an awesome record with the aircraft. Seen here taxying in at McConnell after arriving for the 'Phantom Pharewell' in April 1990, this aircraft looks just as a CO's machine should—absolutely spotless. Carrying a specially commissioned decal on the intake, the groundcrew have even gone as far as to provide the camera ports with customized covers (*Steve Hill*)

Service with the RAF/RN

Besides being the backbone of both the USAF and the US Navy/Marines for the past three decades, the Phantom II has also been a key player with several other air forces across the globe. One of these 'big league' operators has been the Royal Air Force, the British being the first country to order the Phantom II from McDonnell Douglas in 1965. A rather different beast from its counterpart across the 'pond', the RAF/Royal Navy Phantom II had twin Rolls-Royce Spey turbofan engines buried in its fuselage in place of the ubiquitous General Electric J79 turbojets, as well as a Ferranti developed inertial navigation and attack system (INAS) which augmented the AWG-11/12 radar already fitted into the American F-4.

Initially experiencing some problems meeting deadlines and 'Phantomizing' certain components, British industry soon came to grips with the task at hand and supplied St Louis with all the required parts, the first of 118 RAF F-4Ms (later redesignated FGR MK2s) being delivered to No 228 Operational Conversion Unit (OCU) at RAF Coningsby in August 1968. A further 15 frontline squadrons would eventually fly the 'Anglicized' F-4, performing tactical strike, interceptor and reconnaissance duties with it.

Not to be forgotten is the Royal Navy's contribution to the British F-4. The original proponents for the Spey-powered Phantom II, the Navy ordered 52 specially modified F-4Ks (later redesignated FG.MK1s) to replace the ageing Sea Vixens aboard HMS Ark Royal. Introducing an extendable nose oleo leg for optimum incidence catapult launching from the small deck of the 'Ark, and a folding radome to allow it to be struck down to the hangar deck on the vessel's cramped lifts, the first three F-4Ks arrived at Royal Naval Air Station (RNAS) Yeovilton on 19 April 1968. Only two units ever flew the F-4K in Navy colours; No 767 Sqn performing the training function for RN pilots up until it was disbanded in 1972; and No 892 Sqn undertaking all the operational cruises on the 'Ark until it too was disbanded in 1978.

Now a declining breed, the British Phantom II is slowly disappearing from European skies, replaced by an endless procession of Panavia Tornados. Already the FG.1 has been completely retired, and as of 1991 only five frontline units, and the OCU, still fly the FGR.Mk2 and the F-4J(UK), in the air defence role. These too will soon be gone, and the stomach trembling sound of twin-Speys on full afterburner during take-off will be but a fond memory for both aircrews and enthusiasts alike.

Previous pages Viewed from the slightly unorthodox vantage point of the open side door on a SAR Wessex, this FG-1 has just been moved up to waist cat one in preparation for launch. One of the external peculiarities of the British F-4 was the position of the auxiliary air doors on the fuselage, these small flaps invariably staying agape both on the ground and in the air. The reasoning behind this centred on the Rolls-Royce powerplant generating high heat levels in the afterburning section of the engine, these temperatures having not been experienced with the 'cooler' J79. A simple solution was reached; open the auxiliary doors and cool the whole works off with ram air. The third F-4K delivered to the Navy, XT859 gained the distinction of being the first British Phantom II displayed at Farnborough, a crew from the short-lived No 700P Sqn flying it at the 1968 event. Winner of the Atlantic race the following year, XT 859 served with both Nos 767 and 892 before being issued to No 11 Group, RAF Strike Command, in December 1978 (*Mike Vines—Photo Link*)

Right Phantom II deck operations, Royal Navy style. Wearing the familiar Omega on its fin, this No 892 FG.1 is straining at the catapult shuttle, the pilot having selected full afterburner for launch. Participating in HMS Ark Royal's final cruise, the squadron ceased to exist three months after this photo was taken in the Med in October 1978. The flashy red, white and blue marking on the radome stems from the Queen's Royal Jubilee Celebrations of the year before, the squadron badge in the middle of the tricolour replacing a gold crown and the numerals '77'. Maintaining station in the background is a suitably bright search and rescue (SAR) Westland Wessex, performing the 'plane guard' duties for the 'Ark's air wing. In the foreground, wearing their distinctive waistcoats, are the carrier's 'badgers', marine engineers designated by the black stripe as catapult crew. One of the last FG.1s delivered to the Navy, this aircraft (XV589) was delivered to No 767 Sqn in July 1969. Issued to No 892 Sqn in 1972, the Phantom II was eventually transferred to the RAF in December 1978. Joining No 111 Sqn at RAF Leuchars soon after, XV589 was written-off near Alconbury when its radome opened in flight on 3 June 1980 (*Denis J Calvert*)

Left Far more common than their Royal Navy brethren, RAF Phantom IIs had seen exactly a decade's service when this moody photograph was taken in August 1978 at Wildenrath, Germany. Long term residents at this picturesque base near Mönchengladbach, No 19 Sqn, along with fellow F-4 operators No 92 Sqn, are part of the RAF's direct commitment to NATO's fighter force. A squadron with as a rich tradition as any in the RAF, No19 had operated Lightning F.2s and F.2As from Germany since 1965. With the disbandment of RAF Germany's (RAFG) F-4 strike force in 1976, enought surplus Phantom IIs were then available to re-equip the Wildenrath squadrons with relatively fresh aircraft. Sitting cosily in their well-used FGR.2, the crew are just completing their preflight checks before engine spool up (*Ian Black*)

Above Wildenrath in summer can be a beautiful place, the old green and grey camouflage on this No 19 Sqn FGR.2 fitting in nicely with the lush green landscape. The crew will leave their canopies open until they reach the runway to allow the air to circulate around their heavily clad upper torso as, on a warm day like this one, the F-4's inbuilt air conditioning would be hard pressed to keep them cool on the ground. Lacking the radar warning receiver (RWR) box topping on its fin, this aircraft was the eighth FGR.2 delivered to the RAF, going on strength with No 228 OCU in early 1969. Passed on to No 6 Sqn later on that year, the aircraft stayed with this unit until its re-equipment with Jaguars in 1974. On No 19 Sqn books from 1976 to 1982, this aircraft has now gracefully retired (*Ian Black*)

Left Still full of life, an RWR-equipped FGR.2 thunders away from Wildenrath, commencing a dusk patrol over northern Germany, twin afterburners pulsating in the evening sky. Unlike other RAF Phantom II interceptor squadrons back in the UK who are charged with protecting the 'island' from high-level threats, Nos 19 and 92 are trained to 'do the business' at low-level against fast strike aircraft appearing rapidly from across the border. Operating in cramped airspace against some of the hardest targets of all to shoot down, the Wildenrath Phantom IIs have been flown harder, and at lower levels, than any other FGR.2s in the RAF. Perfectly suited to this type of combat, the twin Spey engines give the Phantom II pilots buckets of power to play with in all flight regimes (*Ian Black*)

Above Having completed yet another patrol, the pilot selects gear down and commences his approach into a snow covered Wildenrath in February 1983. Due to their low-level interceptor role, No 19 was one of the last squadrons to operate the Phantom II in the green and grey colours, most other units having adopted the more fashionable air superiority greys by this stage. Streaming wingtip vortices in the chilly air, this particular FGR.2, XT911, was also an ex-No 6 Sqn aircraft (*Ian Black*)

Above Devoid of any stores, bar two inert Sky Flash rounds and a single ACMI telemetry pod on each Sidewinder rail, this 'clean' FGR.2 banks over the German countryside. The ACMI pods allow computers on the ground to track, analyse and store the dogfights that take place between this aircraft and others that are similarly equipped. Perhaps the most important training tool developed in the 1980s, the telemetry pod has taken all the 'ifs' out of fast jet debriefs, and helped sharpen the edge of combat pilots the world over. Looking like a large blade aerial protruding from the port afterburner can, this 'aerodynamic device' actually belongs to the lead-ship in this No 19 Sqn formation (*Ian Black*)

Above right Eventually the squadron 'got with the programme' and resprayed all their aircraft powder grey. Cruising along at a height more frequented by UK-based Phantom II units, this well-worn No 19 Sqn aircraft is carrying both an inert Sky Flash missile (Marconi/EMI modified AIM-7E Sparrow), recessed in the port weapons trough, and an awesome centreline mounted GAU-4 Vulcan cannon, the barrel of which can be seen protruding from the front of its aerodynamic SUU-23/A pod. A formidable weapon that can spit out a full magazine of 1200 high-velocity 20 mm shells in just 12 seconds, the SUU-23/A was developed by McDonnell Douglas in response to lessons learnt in Vietnam by the USAF. A brute of a device which severly shakes the F-4 when a burst is fired, the cannon nevertheless enjoyed marked success with USAF F-4Cs and Ds in the skies over South-east Asia (*Ian Black*)

Right Following a spate of horrific low-level collisions in German airspace in 1988 and early 1989, RAFG decided to try and make their aircraft more visible to aircrews travelling at high speed. Obliterating the 'Dolphin in the Wreath' badge, No 19 Sqn liberally daubed the tail of the CO's aircraft, coded 'AA', with matt black paint. The tail hook is deployed and the orange drums lying beneath the wingtips are plugged into the fuel dump vents to catch any JP4 that may seep from the wing tanks. A well travelled airframe, this FGR.2 was first issued to No 41 Sqn, with whom it served between 1972 and 1977. Spending some time with No 228 OCU after that, the aircraft eventually arrived at Wildenrath in 1988 (*Ian Black*)

Above left Another long-term fighter unit, the famous 'Cocks' of No 43 Sqn flew FG.1s and FGR.2s from RAF Leuchars for 20 years. Maintaining a tight echelon-left formation high above the North Sea, No 43 Sqn (along with No III Sqn) were charged with the responsibility of patrolling the Northern Atlantic and the oil rich North Sea. Often flying in inhospitable weather, the squadrons trained to search out and shoot down enemy bombers at extreme range with Sparrow or Sky Flash missiles. Defending the northern tier of the UK Air Defence Region (UKADR), No 43 Sqn became the first interceptor unit to receive the FG.1 in 1969. Now flying Tornado F3, but still based at Leuchars, the 'Cocks' briefly operated 'newer' FGR.2s in the late 1980s before transitioning onto the Panavia fighter (*Peter Foster*)

Below left Wearing perhaps the most famous squadron badge of all on its nose, this decidedly non-standard RAF Phantom II undergoes preflights by its crew. One of 15 specially refurbished F-4Js pulled from various sources in the US Navy and sold to Britain in 1984, it bears the legendary mark of No 74 'Tiger' Squadron, and is seen basking in the glorious Mediterranean sun during a weapons det to Deci, Sardinia, in May 1990. Powered by standard J79s, and lacking any of the special 'Anglicized' avionics kit, these aircraft nevertheless perform a vital function in defending the middle tier of the UK from their base at RAF Wattisham. Somewhere along the line this aircraft has been 'zapped' by another unidentified 'tiger'squadron, a rather unfriendly looking beast adorning the intake beneath the pale roundel (*Ian Black*)

Above Bought in a straight replacement deal for the FGR.2s that went south to the Falklands with No 23 Sqn (formerly a No 29 Sqn det), the F-4J (UK)s have been flown hard over the past seven years with the minimum of maintenance hassles. Coming from both US Navy and Marine Corps stocks, the aircraft were totally rebuilt before being despatched to Britain. Arriving at Wattisham already resprayed in RAF 'greys', the shade used on the aircraft was somewhat greener than that found on other frontline FGR.2s. On the aircraft closest to the camera only the radome, intake and engine cooling door remain in this unusual shade, the rest of the aircraft having been resprayed during periodic maintenance (*Dennis J Calvert*)

Right With its underside covered in engine fluid, this 'old style' F-4J breaks away from the camera-ship. Carrying a single dummy Sky Flash and an inert, but seeker-head equipped Sidewinder on the port launch rail, this Phantom II is configured in 'playtime' mode, its crew just itching for a spot of dogfighting practice on a fine summer's afternoon in 1990 (*Ian Black*)

Above Turning the clock back seven years to a frosty morning at RAF Wildenrath in February 1983, this hulky FGR.2 slowly taxies out to the runway. Being rather chilly, the crew have decided not to crank the canopies open on this occasion! Carrying the bright checkers of No 92 Sqn on its RWR housing and on either side of the roundel, there is no question as to who owns this jet. Still persisting with green and grey at this late stage, the squadron has had to fit a pale stabilator to this FGR.2, thus adding a new dimension to the scheme on this aircraft. An SUU-23/A 'master blaster' pod is also slung under the fuselage (*Ian Black*)

Above left Just as No 19 Sqn resprayed some of their aircraft with solid colour tails, so too did No 92, although their choice of red better reflects their own personal unit colours. Low-level specialists with the FGR.2 since 1 January 1977, No 92 Sqn continue to enjoy a solid working relationship with their Phantom IIs. Sharing responsibilities equally with No 19 Sqn, the unit maintains a 24-hour, all-year round, Quick Reaction Alert (QRA) pair of Phantom IIs ready to scramble in response to an unknown threat in less than five minutes. Fully armed with live ordnance and plugged into ground starting trolleys, the Battle Flight, or 'Fire Brigade' as they are fondly known at Wildenrath, is fully manned by permanently kitted up crews ready to go on the command of their sector controller. Not on a 'Zulu' alert this time, however, this brightly painted machine has previously served in the colours of Nos 11, 31, 2 and 56 Sqns respectively during a hectic career (*Ian Black*)

Below left Also sprayed up in high viz colours, but this time in blue, XV498 sits fully armed in a protective revetment at Wildenrath. Stretching the blue across the canopies, this particular FGR.2 has recently been resprayed judging by the slightly shiny finish to the paint. Carrying a pair of AIM-9Ls on each Sidewinder pylon, four Sky Flash missiles recessed in the fuselage and an SUU-23/A gun pod on the centreline station, this aircraft is ready for anything— as long as the radius of acton is moderate! Having served at Port Stanley in the Falkland Islands for some time, this late-build FGR.2 is still currently on strength with No 92 Sqn (*Ian Black*)

Above Getting their first taste of high performance interceptors with the thundering English Electric Lightning, No 111 Sqn (or Treble One as they are known in the RAF) entered the FGR.2 world on 30 September 1974 at RAF Coningsby. A year later they moved to their present home at RAF Leuchars, in the wilds of Scotland. Up until 1990 they flew the Phantom II in the air defence role, and then like No 43 Sqn, the boys at 'Treble One' transitioned onto the supersonic 'flick-knife', the Tornado F.3. This classic and extremely rare shot, taken in August 1984, was specially staged by the squadron to show all three types of scheme currently in use at the time. The first two aircraft wear standard colours, but the third is marked up with special old style roundels and a large rudder tricolour for its participation in the 1983 Air Tattoo at Greenham Common. As the serials state, all three aircraft are FG.1s, No 111 Sqn transitioning on to this mark in 1979 to help simplify engineering support at the base (*Denis J Calvert*)

Above The 'student' and the 'instructor'. Flying in a neat formation high above the North Sea, a Treble One crew close in on an 'electric' Canberra T Mk.17 from the joint services RN/RAF No 360 Sqn at RAF Wyton. Jammed packed with electronic signals equipment, the Canberras fly endless sorties for the Leuchars squadrons emitting various jamming frequencies as they cruise around the skies. The Phantom II crews have to somehow combat this 'beam bending' mess and intercept the Canberra, or whatever else the No 360 Sqn aircraft happens to be hiding (*Tim Laming*)

Right Painted up in late 1989 to celebrate the Phantom II's retirement from service with Treble One, 'Black Mike', a veteran FG.1, was the star of many airshows during the 1990 season. Completely stripped back to bare metal and then resprayed in gloss black, the aircraft certainly looked impressive, although the camouflage qualities of the scheme were questionable! To add the finishing touch, the maintenance shop at Leuchars had two dummy Sky Flash rounds sprayed up and fitted beneath the aircraft (*Ian Black*)

All ex-Fleet Air Arm aircraft, and all now shore-based in Scotland, a pair of FG.1s formate with a single S.2B Buccaneer from No 12 Sqn. Devoid of any unit markings, the rear Phantom II had only recently arrived on the squadron when this shot was taken in December 1987. Based at nearby RAF Lossiemouth, the Buccaneers would expect to receive top cover from Treble One if they were called upon to perform a ship strike in the Atlantic or North Sea. Despite wearing a No 208 Sqn chevron on the nose, the photographer is adamant that this Buccaneer belongs to No 12 Sqn *(Denis J Calvert)*

The first unit to receive the FGR.2 in RAF service was No 228 Operational Conversion Unit (OCU) at Coningsby on 23 August 1968. When this photo was taken almost 22 years later at Boscombe Down, the squadron was still flying the venerable 'Big Ugly'. Wearing the markings of No 64 Sqn 'shadow' on its intake, this aircraft is parked on the 'live' ramp at the Buckinghamshire base during the Battle of Britain Airshow weekend. Nominated as the 'spare' aircraft, this FGR.2 was ready to perform the airshow routine flown by the Phantom II parked behind it had there been a technical glitch with that machine. Everything went smoothly however, and the crew, preparing their mount in the background, put on an outstanding performance (*John Dibbs*)

Above left Photographed on a wet and windy August day over the former Battle of Britain base at West Malling, this FGR.2, the third-last RAF Phantom II built, was not long for this earth. Less than a month after the shot was taken in 1988, the crew of this No 228 OCU FGR.2 failed to recover from a tight loop over RAF Abingdon's main runway and were killed when XV499 hit the ground (*John Dibbs*)

Below left Showing off the aircraft's low speed abilities, the 1990 display crew from No 228 OCU lazily crab the Phantom II from side to side down the runway at the Mildenhall Air Fete. Letting it all hang out, the probe is visible extended behind the cockpit and the nose gear is stretched to its maximum length. Flying the 'spare' on this occasion, the crew are strapped into XT900, the aircraft featured in the Boscombe Down photograph (*John Dibbs*)

Above Same routine but photographed just as the pilot kicks in the afterburner and climbs away into his next manoeuvre. One of the finest displays put on by an RAF Phantom II crew, the instructor pair of Flt Lt Steve Howard and Flt Lt Nige Marks from Coningsby have been flying the airshow circuit for several seasons (*John Dibbs*)

Cruising over the Forth of Tay on approach to Leuchars, the pilot has selected gear down and has extended the slats to give the aircraft that extra bite into the air stream as it slows down for landing. Still flown by the boss at the OCU, XT900 now carries Wing Commander Walmsley's name on the front canopy rail, and Squadron Leader Kirk's on the rear. Designated a 'shadow' squadron, the OCU would be manned by its instructors and support other frontline units as No 64 Sqn in the central tier of the UKADR during a crisis (*Robbie Shaw*)

The pit of the stomach reverberates and the brain bounces around as an FGR.2 pilot selects phase five afterburner for a scorching departure at the 1983 Air Tattoo at Greenham Common. Carrying a full weapons load and no tanks, this aircraft should unstick from the long 'Common blacktop in rather impressive fashion. Photographed at about the time when most RAF Phantom IIs were being resprayed, the finish on this aircraft suggests that it may have recently visited the Coningsby paint shop (*Robbie Shaw*)

Left Silhouetted against the Forth of Firth, this blue-tailed aircraft is the CO's FGR.2, and is coded accordingly. The same Phantom II as featured in the photos taken at Mildenhall, it was resprayed soon after this shot was taken in December 1988. Having served with No 14 Sqn in Germany for five years, the aircraft returned to Britain and was placed in storage after its former owners began to receive their first Jaguars in 1976. Issued to the OCU in 1982, the veteran FGR.2 has trained many a pilot and navigator over the years (*Robbie Shaw*)

Above Easily the brightest FG.1 ever to wear a British roundel, this particular aircraft is also the oldest Phantom II still regularly flying in the UK. The third airframe delivered, it never actually saw service with either the RAF or the RN, being issued to the Aeroplane and Armament Experimental Establishment (A&AEE) at Boscombe Down to perform development work for the overall UK Phantom II programme. Photographed at Greenham Common some 15 years after it had first arrived in Britain, this aircraft was the star of the 1983 Air Tattoo, carry special decals to celebrate the 25th anniversary of the Phantom II. The overall red, white and blue scheme is worn on all A&AEE Ministry of Defence (MoD) aircraft (*Robbie Shaw*)

Under other Flags

A total of 5201 F-4 Phantom IIs were built in a time frame encompassing 25 years. Of that impressive figure, 5074 first took to the skies from Lambert Field, Missouri, having been shaped from raw steel at McDonnell Douglas' legendary St Louis plant. However, the very last Phantom II to tuck its gear up and accelerate away from terra firma for the first time did so at a location well over 5000 miles away from the black top at Lambert Field. Wearing the serial 17-8440 on its fin, this F-4EJ left the Mitsubishi factory at Nagoya in 1981 without any pomp or ceremony, bound for service with the Japanese Air Self-Defense Force (JASDF). Thus an important, and considerably 'thick' chapter in military aviation history was brought to a close.

As we enter the 1990s, 11 nations still operate F-4s across the globe. Britain was the first customer (as detailed in the previous chapter), but they were soon followed by Iran, whose Air Force would eventually receive 225 F-4s. Used tirelessly during the bloody war with Iraq, very few Phantom IIs now still serve due to a chronic shortage of spare parts. Another seasoned user of the F-4 in the Middle East is Israel, this small nation receiving 204 F-4Es and 12 RF-4Es during the early 1970s. Heavily used in both the 1973 Yom Kippur War and the Lebanese invasion in 1982, the Israeli Phantom II squadrons have been the backbone of the Air Defense Force for almost two decades. Staying in the region, Egypt received 35 F-4Es from the USAF's 31st TFW in 1979 during *Operation Peace Pharaoh*, their delivery being viewed in the west as a sign of the nation's break with their former military suppliers, the Soviet Union. The last customer for the Phantom II, the Egyptians initially experienced severe problems keeping these highly complex aircraft flying. Moving into Europe, the F-4 has found favour with four NATO forces, besides the RAF. Starting with the first and largest user of the aircraft, the West Germans received their initial batch of RF-4Es in January 1971. After receiving 88 recce-Phantom IIs, the Luftwaffe then ordered no less than 177 F-4Fs, these aircraft being very similar to the USAF's E-models. Soon after the Germans received their first RF-4s, the smallest Phantom II operators in NATO, Spain, commenced operations with 36 F-4Cs and four RF-4Cs.

Sharing a common, but icy, border at the opposite end of the Mediterranean are two more 'Phantom Phlyers', Greece and Turkey. Delivered between 1974 and 1978, 56 F-4Es and eight RF-4Es were taken on strength by three squadrons in the Hellenic Air Force, and unlike their Turkish counterparts, all these aircraft were fresh from the St Louis production line. Just as they have done with the F-104 Starfighter, and the F-84 Thunderstreak before that, the Turks are currently buying up second-hand F-4Es from the USAF and Spain at an astonishing rate. At present seven squadrons share 130 F-4Es and eight RF-4Es. Eighty of these aircraft were purchased brand new from St Louis in the mid 1970s.

Moving half way across the globe, a sizeable force of F-4Ds, Es and RF-4Cs are operated by the Republic of Korea Air Force (ROKAF). Ending where we began with the Japanese, the Nagoya plant delivered 125 F-4EJs and 14 RF-4EJs to the JASDF. Operating a large modern fleet of Phantom IIs, the Japanese will undoubtedly be one of the last nations to retire the F-4 from frontline service sometime in the next century.

Previous pages Assigned to the Western Air Defense Command and based at Tsuiki, this impressive line up of F-4EJs belongs to the 304th Hikotai (Squadron)/8th Kokudan (Wing), and as with everything Japanese, these aircraft are kept in spotless condition, Because of the defensive role required by Japan's constitution, the F-4s were originally delivered by Mitsubishi without air-to-air refuelling capability. However, they have since been retrofitted with refuelling receptacles which allow the squadrons to take advantage of the large USAF tanker fleet in the Pacific. Most Japanese Phantom IIs were delivered in this gull grey and white scheme, reminiscent of the colours worn on US Navy F-4s (*Peter R Foster*)

Above Someway from home, this rather tired looking F-4E was one of 36 Phantom IIs supplied to Egypt during *Operation Peace Pharaoh* in 1979. With its national insignia obliterated, but still wearing the rapid identification bars on the fin and spine, this early production aircraft was photographed at McGuire AFB during a stopover on its way to Texas for heavy depot maintenance on 24 August 1989. Having served with the

USAF since 1968, this aircraft was totally refurbished before it was despatched to Cairo West AB to serve with the 222nd Fighter Regiment. Unfortunately for the aircraft concerned, Egyptian maintenance personnel received no formal training on the Phantom II's systems before they arrived, this resulting in as many as 27 F-4s being unservicable at one point. Things have picked up as the years have progressed though and the aircraft are now an integral part of the Egyptian Air Force (*Barry Roop via David F Brown*)

Below right A 'rare bird' in the JASDF, a distinctively badged 501st Hikotai RF-4EJ approaches the main strip at Hyakuri AB in May 1990. Only 14 recce-Phantom IIs were delivered to the Defense Force between November 1974 and June 1975 to equip a solitary squadron. Originally wearing the standard 'EJ grey over white, the 501st evaluated several different schemes in the early eighties before adopting this rich overall finish. Soon to be retired from service, the surviving 11 recce-Phantom IIs are to be replaced by 17 newer F-4EJs converted to RF-4 standard with a Thomson-CSF Raphael sideways-looking airborne radar (SLAR) (*Robbie Shaw*)

Above right Moving further up the main Japanese island to the prefecture of the Central Air Defense Command, this F-4EJ belongs to the 305th Hikotai/7th Kokudan at Hyakuri Air Base. Operating alongside another Japanese-built McDonnell Douglas product, the F-15J Eagle, the Phantom II force is currently being extensively upgraded to *Kai* standards. The modifications include increasing the airframe life from 3000 to 5000 hours; installing a new look-down APG-66J radar, which is linked to a new central computer, Head up Display (HUD) and Litton LN-39 intertial navigation system (INS); and fitting a JAPR-4 *Kai* RWR set. These improvements will allow the F-4EJ *Kai* to carry the Mitsubishi ASM-1 anti-ship missile, as well as both the AIM-7F and AIM-9L. A total of 96 airframes are involved in this programme (*Robbie Shaw*)

Left Unique amongst Phantom II operators in being the only non-American users of the F-4C, the Ejercito del Air (Spanish Air Force) received their first aircraft in October 1971. Receiving a total of 44 F-4Cs (including four attrition replacements) and 4 RF-4Cs, all the Spanish aircraft had previously seen service with the USAF. Once viewed as possible F-4E customers, the Spanish received the C-models as part of an inter-government deal covering US military use of bases in the country. For a long time part of NATO's 5th Allied Tactical Air Force, both F-4C-equipped squadrons recently retired their aircraft and received brand new Spanish-built EF-18 Hornets in their place. Seen here landing at Torrejon AB on 3 May 1988, this aircraft wears the distinctive lynx head badge of Ala de Caza 12 on its fin. Both Escuadron 121 and 122 were based at Torrejon and controlled by Ala de Caza 12 (*Peter R Foster*)

Above Wearing a shade of blue not too far removed from the colour of the sky behind it, this heavily 'plumbed' F-4E of the Greek Air Force sits on the ramp at RAF Coltishall in July 1990. Belonging to No 339 Mira (Squadron) No 117 Pterix (Wing), this aircraft is normally based at Larissa in north-eastern Greece. However, as part of a unit exhange with No 6 Sqn, who fly Jaguars, two F-4Es transitted across from the Mediterranean to the RAF station in Norfolk. Formerly an F-84F Thunderstreak unit, No 339 Mira received their first F-4s in late 1974 as part of a general upgrading of the Air Force that took place when the first Phantom IIs arrived. Four units fly F-4s in Greek service; two in the air defence role, one in the strike role and one tasked with reconnaissance duties, flying a small batch of RF-4Es. The Greek government recently signed a deal with their US counterparts which will see up to 50 surplus F-4Es transferred to the Hellenic Air Force over the next two years (*Bob Archer*)

Right Not too many miles away from Greece can be found more F-4Es, but this time decorated with red and white roundels instead of blue and white ones. Rolling out of its hardened shelter past decoy F-84s, this F-4E belongs to the 112th Filo (Squadron) at Eskisehir Air Base. One of the new-build aircraft delivered from St Louis, this F-4E also happened to be the 4995 airframe completed at the McDonnell Douglas plant. Flown hard by the Turks, and beginning to show its age, this aircraft is still a relative youngster when compared to most F-4s, having only beeen delivered in 1978 (*Robbie Shaw*)

Above Ten years older than the previous Turkish F-4E, this aircraft, seen here during NATO exercise *Display Determination* '86, had already seen many years of service wearing 'stars and bars' before being transferred to the Turks in 1985. With its tailcone open and parachute laying discarded on the grass in front of it, the Phantom II has just returned from a sortie over the Turkish coast. Also a 112th Filo aircraft, this F-4 is seen here forward deployed to Bandirma AB (*Yves Debay*)

The second of eight RF-4Es delivered to the
Turkish Air Force, this smart looking
machine is 'cooling off' on the Eskisehir
ramp after a hard day's flying in November
1985. As with the F-4E, the RF version had
the wing leading-edge slats fitted to it, the
starboard device clearly visible in this
photo. Officially only equipped with eight
airframes, the sole Phantom II recce unit,
113 Filo, will undoubtedly be hoping that
some second-hand RF-4s might come their
way soon (Robbie Shaw)

Although being rapidly approached by the Turks, the Luftwaffe are still the largest users of the Phantom II outside of the USAF. Maintaining a smart echelon left formation away from the camera-ship, these F-4Fs wear the distinctive badge of Jagdbombergeschwader (JBG) 35, one of two fighter-bomber wings equipped with the Phantom II. Based at Pferasfeld, the 'mud-moving' F-4s are not usually seen at this height (*Robbie Shaw*)

Above left The second fighter-attack wing equiped with the F-4F is seen on the ramp during a weapons deployment to Goose Bay in Canada. JBG 36 are also based at Pfersfeld and received their first F-4Fs soon after JBG 35. Like many NATO countries, the Luftwaffe often send their Phantom II and Tornado units across the Atlantic to Goose Bay for low-level bombing training. Unlike the F-4s in the previous photo which still wore the original delivery scheme, these aircraft wear the new blend of soft greys overall. The green stabilator and spine flashed on the first two aircraft act as visual aids to ground controllers out on the ranges at 'Goose' (*Fritz Becker via David F Brown*)

Left High above the clouds on patrol, this pair of JG 74 aircraft are totally devoid of any stores, although they both carry the almost mandatory inboard pylons with Sidewinder rails affixed. As with the fighter/bomber units, both JG 71 and 74 have 'greyed out' their F-4Fs since this photo was taken in November 1982 (*Ian Black*)

Above Wearing the name of one of the greatest German fighter aces of all time on its intake, a JG 74 'Molders' F-4F waits for its pilot and WSO to strap in before going aloft. Along with the similarly equipped JG 71 'Richthofen', JG 74 are responsible for the air defence of Germany, with a little help from USAFE and RAFG of course! The F-4F is fully wired up to carry the medium range AIM-7 Sparrow missile, although the Germans chose not to purchase this weapon, and have equipped their aircraft with the Sidewinder only (*Ian Black*)

Specially decorated to celebrate the 25th anniversary of the reformation of JG 74, this garish F-4F was on strength with the wing at Wittmundhafen for most of 1986. Just as the Japanese are upgrading their Phantom IIs, so too are the Germans, a two tier programme known as ICE (Improved Combat Efficiency) extending the life of the fleet up to the year 2005. The first part of ICE will see the aircraft structurally strengthened and equipped with new navigational attack equipment. The second phase, which affects 109 interceptor-tasked F-4Fs only, will see the new APQ-120 'look-down' radar fitted and the aircraft made compatible with the Hughes AIM-120A Advanced Medium Range Air-to-Air Missile (AMRAAM) (*Ian Black*)

Having only just arrived that afternoon for the Battle of Britain Airshow at Boscombe Down, a drab RF-4E from Aufklarungsgeschwader (AKG) 52 sits amongst the puddles, awaiting the next shower on a cold June afternoon in 1990. Charged with the responsibility of performing a fair slab of NATO's tactical reconnaissance requirements, both AKG 51 at Bremgarten and AKG 52 at Leck operate large numbers of RF-4Es. Essentially similar to the USAF's RF-4Cs, the Luftwaffe aircraft can, however, tote up to 5000 lbs of bombs under their wings if the need arose (*Tony Holmes*)

Overleaf Completing a JP4 transaction high above the Atlantic, an AKG 52 RF-4 is firmly plugged into a KC-135. Just discernable through the canopy is the pilot's international orange flight suit, this brightly coloured garment once being standard issue with many air forces around the world. Now considered too bright for safety in the low-viz world of fast jets, many German and Japanese F-4 crews still wear them nevertheless (*Robbie Shaw*)